The Progressive Movement 1900–1920
Efforts to Reform America's New Industrial Society ™

WOMEN'S SUFFRAGE

Giving the Right to Vote to All Americans

Jennifer MacBain-Stephens

rosen central
Primary Source ™

The Rosen Publishing Group, Inc., New York

For my mother, Nan Bailey

Published in 2006 by The Rosen Publishing Group, Inc.
29 East 21st Street, New York, NY 10010

First Edition

Library of Congress Cataloging-in-Publication Data

MacBain-Stephens, Jennifer.
Women's suffrage: giving the right to vote to all Americans / by Jennifer MacBain-Stephens.
    p. cm. — (The Progressive movement, 1900–1920: efforts to reform America's new industrial society)
Includes bibliographical references and index.
ISBN 1-4042-0199-8 (lib. bdg.)
ISBN 1-4042-0869-0 (pbk. bdg.)
6-pack ISBN 1-4042-6197-4
1. Women—Suffrage—United States—Juvenile literature. I. Title. II. Series: Progressive movement.
JK1898.M33 2004
324.6'23'0973—dc22

                                                              2004000753

Manufactured in the United States of America

On the Cover: Top: Women in New York City cast votes in 1920; Bottom: Suffragists march in New York City in 1913.

Photo credits: cover (top), pp. 5, 26 © Bettmann/Corbis, cover (bottom), pp. 7 (right), 11, 19, 23, 24 (left) Library of Congress Prints and Photographs Division; p. 7 (left) Courtesy of Smithsonian Institution Libraries, Washington, DC; p. 8 Courtesy of Mount Holyoke College Archives and Special Collections, South Hadley, MA; pp. 10, 13 Library of Congress Manuscript Division; p. 16 National Archives; p. 17 Bryn Mawr College Library; p. 21 The Schlesinger Library, Radcliffe Institute, Harvard University; p. 24 (right) Wisconsin Historical Society.

Designer: Les Kanturek; Editor: Mark Beyer; Photo Researcher: Amy Feinberg

Contents

Chapter One

Before Women Had Voting Rights

In the United States, women who are eighteen years or older can vote. They can vote for mayors, governors, Congress members, and the president of the United States. Voting is, perhaps, a liberty that many women think has always been open to them. But this is not true. Women only gained the right to vote in the twentieth century. And they did so after a hard and long struggle against the state and federal governments. Before then, women could not vote in general elections simply because they were women.

Women's suffrage, or the right to vote, was won on August 26, 1920. On that day a constitutional amendment was approved. It granted women full suffrage in the United States.

However, it was a long and difficult road leading up to the year 1920. Women were fighting for the vote during the

Progressive reformists included women demanding the right to vote. After nearly eighty years of trying without success, women gained voting rights in general elections in 1920. These suffragettes *(above)* celebrate the passing of the Nineteenth Amendment, which made it unlawful to deny the right to vote based on gender.

entire Progressive movement and long before that period. The Progressive movement was an era of great reform from 1900 to 1920. Great changes in political, social, and economic ideas took place in America during these years. People understood the power of large businesses and how they were often corrupt. People demanded rights for the farmer and the basic needs of the consumer. Child labor, dirty living conditions, dangerous workplaces, and long working hours were called into question. Many reforms included the Pure Food and Drug Act, the Meat Inspection Act, and the passage of several constitutional amendments.

What was life like in the United States when it was a given that women should not vote? Between the early 1800s and the Civil War (1861–1865), there was a rising middle class in the United States. This class included families in which the men worked as office managers, business owners, lawyers, and teachers. The men worked and the women stayed at home with the children. This family was considered the "backbone" of society.

Men going into the work world created stereotypical ideas about the roles of men and women in America at this time. Later, historians would call this time the "cult of domesticity." These ideas were discussed in many advice manuals, sermons, poems, and even medical essays. It was thought that men alone should deal with the harsh events of the rough work world and women should rarely leave the home. Women were thought to be physically weak and pure of heart. At this time, until around 1880, the ideal

Womanhood in the early nineteenth century meant living happily in the home, raising children, and serving one's husband. Pamphlets, such as the one shown above *(left)*, and books were printed to teach women how to be good in this role. Real life never lived up to the image, however. Women wanted a more dynamic life outside the home.

woman developed four parts of her life: purity, domesticity, piety, and submissiveness. Women were expected to uphold certain values in the home (stability and morality). Women were also supposed to create an escape for their husbands from the competitive business world.

Mary Lyon helped lift women out of the role of housewife and maid and into the world of knowledge and professional work. She founded Mount Holyoke College in 1837.

Women's groups and colleges slowly started to change this ideal of womanhood. In 1833, Oberlin College in Ohio awarded its first academic degrees to three female students. In 1836, Sarah Grimke began a speaking career as an abolitionist (someone against slavery). She was eventually silenced by male abolitionists who thought her public talks were hurting their cause. In 1837, the first National Female Anti-Slavery Society convention met in New York. Also in 1837, Mary Lyon founded Mount Holyoke College in Massachusetts. Years later Mount Holyoke became the first four-year university devoted to women's education in America.

In 1839, the state of Mississippi passed the first Married Woman's Property Act. This act allowed a legally separated wife to keep what she had earned during the marriage. It was a meeting in London, England, in 1840, however, that would change women's rights forever.

Chapter Two

The Demand for Suffrage

In 1840, two ladies, along with their husbands, traveled to London as delegates to the World Anti-Slavery Convention. These two women were Lucretia Mott and Elizabeth Cady Stanton. Stanton met Mott at the convention for the first time. They were shocked to discover that because they were female, they could not join in the debates (nor could the British women who were there). Stanton, Mott, and the other women present were forced to sit outside the debate room. Later, Lucretia Mott wrote in her diary that the "world" convention was titled as such by "mere poetic license." The angry women sat and promised to do something about this mistreatment. Stanton poured her anger into a plan. She wrote in her own diary, "We resolved to hold a convention as soon as we returned home, and form a society to advocate the rights of women."

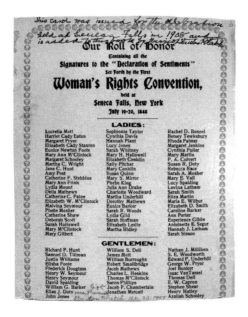

This card was issued for the celebration held at Seneca Falls in 1908 and is added to the list...

Our Roll of Honor

Containing all the

Signatures to the "Declaration of Sentiments"

Set Forth by the First

Woman's Rights Convention,

held at

Seneca Falls, New York

July 19-20, 1848

LADIES:

Lucretia Mott	Sophronia Taylor	Rachel D. Bonnel
Harriet Cady Eaton	Cynthia Davis	Betsey Tewksbury
Margaret Pryor	Hannah Plant	Rhoda Palmer
Elizabeth Cady Stanton	Lucy Jones	Margaret Jenkins
Eunice Newton Foote	Sarah Whitney	Cynthia Fuller
Mary Ann M'Clintock	Mary H. Hallowell	Mary Martin
Margaret Schooley	Elizabeth Conklin	P. A. Culvert
Martha C. Wright	Sally Pitcher	Susan R. Doty
Jane C. Hunt	Mary Conklin	Rebecca Race
Amy Post	Susan Quinn	Sarah A. Mosher
Catherine F. Stebbins	Mary S. Mirror	Mary E. Vail
Mary Ann Frink	Phebe King	Lucy Spalding
Lydia Mount	Julia Ann Drake	Lovina Latham
Delia Mathews	Charlotte Woodward	Sarah Smith
Catherine C. Paine	Martha Underhill	Eliza Martin
Elizabeth W. M'Clintock	Dorothy Mathews	Maria E. Wilbur
Malvina Seymour	Eunice Barker	Elizabeth D. Smith
Phebe Mosher	Sarah R. Woods	Caroline Barker
Catherine Shaw	Lydia Gild	Ann Porter
Deborah Scott	Sarah Hoffman	Experience Gibbs
Sarah Hallowell	Elizabeth Leslie	Antoinette E. Segur
Mary M'Clintock	Martha Ridley	Hannah J. Latham
Mary Gilbert		Sarah Sisson

GENTLEMEN:

Richard P. Hunt	William S. Dell	Nathan J. Milliken
Samuel D. Tillman	James Mott	S. E. Woodworth
Justin Williams	William Burroughs	Edward F. Underhill
Elisha Foote	Robert Smallbridge	George W. Pryor
Frederick Douglass	Jacob Mathews	Joel Bunker
Henry W. Seymour	Charles L. Hoskins	Isaac Van Tassel
Henry Seymour	Thomas M'Clintock	Thomas Dell
David Spalding	Saron Phillips	E. W. Capron
William G. Barker	Jacob P. Chamberlain	Stephen Shear
Elias J. Doty	Jonathan Metcalf	Henry Hatley
John Jones		Azaliah Schooley

These signatures on the Declaration of Sentiments at the Woman's Rights Convention showed the country that both women and men demanded equal voting rights for all citizens.

Before Stanton met with Mott again, she wrote her Declaration of Sentiments. This document, based on the Declaration of Independence, declared the rights of women. When Stanton showed her document to her husband, Henry, he was not happy. He told her that if she ever showed the document in public, he would leave town.

Finally, on July 19 and 20 in 1848, Stanton read her Declaration of Sentiments at the now-famous Woman's Rights Convention at Seneca Falls in New York. The declaration listed several resolutions. One of them was that no man shall withhold a woman's rights, take her property

Lucretia Mott *(left)* became famous for standing up against discrimination toward women when she helped hold the Woman's Rights Convention in Seneca Falls, New York, in 1848. Elizabeth Cady Stanton *(right, seated)* wrote the famous Declaration of Sentiments. Susan B. Anthony *(right, standing)* joined the movement in 1852 and worked for the rest of her life for women's suffrage.

away, or refuse her the ability to vote. Three hundred people argued and discussed the resolutions. Most of the statements received support. The women signed the document. Unfortunately, the press and religious leaders looked down

Pioneer of the Suffrage Movement

Elizabeth Cady Stanton (1815–1902) is believed to be the first leader in the women's rights movement. Stanton wrote most of the movement's documents.

Stanton and Matilda Joslyn Gage wrote the Declaration of Rights of the Women of the United States, which Susan B. Anthony presented, uninvited, at the 1876 centennial party in Washington, D.C. Later in her career, Stanton focused on other social reforms for women. She also worked on the book *The Woman's Bible*.

on the convention. They thought it was not a woman's place to vote, or be arguing for rights the majority did not want to give. One newspaper report supported the document and convention. This was the *North Star*, owned by the escaped slave Frederick Douglass.

In 1852, Susan B. Anthony, a teacher and an acquaintance of Stanton's, joined the women's movement. Anthony dedicated her life to women's suffrage and abolitionism. For the next few years, Anthony traveled across the country and lectured. She called out for women to win the vote. In 1863, Anthony and Stanton organized the Women's National Loyal League. This

THE NORTH STAR.

ROCHESTER, JULY 28, 1848.

The Rights of Women.

One of the most interesting events of the past week, was the holding of what is technically styled a Woman's Rights Convention, at Seneca Falls. The speaking, addresses, and resolutions of this extraordinary meeting, were almost wholly conducted by women; and although they evidently felt themselves in a novel position, it is but simple justice to say, that their whole proceedings were characterized by marked ability and dignity. No one present, we think, however much he might be disposed to differ from the views advanced by the leading speakers on that occasion, will fail to give them credit for brilliant talents and excellent dispositions. In this meeting, as in other deliberative assemblies, there were frequently differences of opinion and animated discussion; but in no case was there the slightest absence of good feeling and decorum. Several interesting documents, setting forth the rights as well as the grievances of woman, were read. Among these was a declaration of sentiments, to be regarded as the basis of a grand movement for attaining all the civil, social, political and religious rights of woman. As these documents are soon to be published in pamphlet form, under the authority of a Committee of women, appointed by that meeting, we will not mar them by attempting any synopsis of their contents. We should not, however, do justice to our own convictions, or to the excellent persons connected with this infant movement, if we did not, in this connection, offer a few remarks on the general subject which

against us the fury of bigotry and the folly of prejudice. A discussion of the rights of animals would be regarded with far more complacency by many of what are called the wise and the good of our land, than would be a discussion of the rights of woman. It is, in their estimation, to be guilty of evil thoughts, to think that woman is entitled to rights equal with man. Many who have at last made the discovery that negroes have some rights as well as other members of the human family, have yet to be convinced that woman is entitled to any. Eight years ago, a number of persons of this description actually abandoned the anti-slavery cause, lest by giving their influence in that direction, they might possibly be giving countenance to the dangerous heresy that woman, in respect to rights, stands on an equal footing with man. In the judgment of such persons, the American slave system, with all its concomitant horrors, is less to be deplored than this *wicked* idea. It is perhaps needless to say, that we cherish little sympathy for such sentiments, or respect for such prejudices. Standing as we do upon the watch-tower of human freedom, we cannot be deterred from an expression of our approbation of any movement, however humble, to improve and elevate the character and condition of any members of the human family. While it is impossible for us to go into this subject at length, and dispose of the various objections which are often urged against such a doctrine as that of female equality, we are free to say, that in respect to political rights, we hold woman to be justly entitled to all we claim for man. We go farther, and express our conviction that all political rights which it is expedient for man to exercise, it is equally so for woman. All that distinguishes man as an intelligent and ac-

tering the laws of the land. Our doctrine is, that "Right is of no sex." We therefore bid the women engaged in this movement our humble God-speed.

The Woman's Rights Convention gained national recognition in the newspapers. Many papers agreed with women's struggles. There were many people who thought, however, that women leaving the home, or even voting, would harm the nation.

Harriet Tubman

Born in 1819 or 1820 as Harriet Ross, this runaway slave learned to stand up for herself. Harriet Ross became Harriet Tubman after she married. Tubman escaped from slavery in 1849. Over the next ten years, she put herself in danger and helped about 300 slaves escape from the South.

During the Civil War, Tubman served as a nurse, a spy, and even a soldier. At the close of the war, Tubman settled in Auburn, New York, which was only twelve miles (nineteen kilometers) away from Seneca Falls, site of the famous Woman's Rights Convention. Tubman supported women's suffrage in her area and spoke about it publicly. The Harriet Tubman Home stands in Auburn, New York, to this day.

league supported the Thirteenth Amendment, which outlawed slavery. Slavery was abolished, or made illegal, in 1864 when Abraham Lincoln signed the Emancipation Proclamation. Slavery was the first major victory for national groups working to change government. They went on to campaign for blacks and women's full citizenship at the same time.

Chapter Three

Organizing for Change

I n 1866, Stanton and Anthony started the American Equal Rights Association along with other famous suffragettes, Lucretia Mott and Lucy Stone. Disagreements about association policies split up the group. Some women felt they should put their "right to vote" aside and campaign for black freedom first. Stanton and Anthony had a falling out with Frederick Douglass. In the campaign for Kansas governor in 1867, the two women had the support of a Democratic businessman, George Train, who was against African American freedom but supported women's suffrage. Some suffragettes thought that Stanton and Anthony were becoming too radical.

In 1869, Stanton and Anthony formed an organization called the National Woman Suffrage Association (NWSA). The NWSA supported an easier divorce process for women

A PETITION
FOR
UNIVERSAL SUFFRAGE.

Stanton, Anthony, and other activists petitioned Congress for universal suffrage in January 1866. They asked that an amendment to the United States Constitution be passed so that all women in the country would have the right to vote.

and called for an end to inequality between men and women in employment and pay. The NWSA supported the unionization of women workers, and it supported the first female presidential candidate, Victoria Woodhull.

In contrast to the NWSA, another group was created in that same year—the American Woman Suffrage Association (AWSA)—headed by Lucy Stone, Julia Ward Howe, and Josephine Ruffin. The AWSA was less radical than the NWSA. It sided with the Republican Party and wanted only to get women the right to vote. It did not focus on any other issues.

In 1870, the AWSA founded its own magazine, the *Women's Journal*. This journal featured columns by the members and was edited by Lucy Stone. It also had cartoons illustrated by Blanche Ames, Lou Rogers, Fredrikke Palmer,

Group of State Presidents and Officers of the N.A.W.S.A. at Nat. Convention, 1892.

1. Mrs. Jean Greenleaf, Pres. N.Y. Assn. 4. Isabella Beecher Hooker, Pres. Conn. Assn. 7. Anna Howard Shaw, Nat. V. Pres. 28 Clara B. Colby, Ed. Woman's Tribune.

By 1892, the National American Woman Suffrage Association had chapters in every state. This photo shows the state presidents and officers of the national movement to get an amendment added to the Constitution.

and Mary Sigsbee. Other regional groups of the AWSA printed political journals such as the *Women Voter* and *Maryland Suffrage News*.

Also in 1870, both the NWSA and the AWSA protested the Fifteenth Amendment, which Congress passed. This gave former male slaves the right to vote. Women could not

Sister Movement in England

In Britain in 1903, Emmeline Pankhurst started the Women's Social and Political Union (WSPU) along with her daughters Christabel and Sylvia. During the summer of 1908, the WSPU started breaking windows in government buildings. Twenty-seven women were arrested when they threw stones through the windows of the prime minister's home. Once in jail, many women went on hunger strikes.

Members of the WSPU were called suffragettes and the nation was shocked that these women used violence to get their point across. During the summer of 1913, suffragettes tried to burn down the houses of two members of the government who opposed women obtaining the vote. From there, they tried to burn down cricket pavilions and golf houses. Some women leaders in the WSPU disagreed with the arson campaign. Those who disagreed were often dismissed.

understand why they, too, could not get the right to vote. They felt like second-class citizens in their own country.

After the 1872 election, the differing political opinions between the two groups began to fade. There were discussions about combining the two groups into one association. Together they could fight the same fight. There was so much hostility, however, that the two groups

Women in Britain fought for the vote using harsher measures. Those sent to prison for protesting went on hunger strikes. The government tried to force-feed these women. The Women's Social and Political Union used posters like this one to tell the people what their government was doing to women in the prisons.

did not merge until 1890. In 1890, the two suffrage groups joined to form the National American Woman Suffrage Association (NAWSA). Everyone worked together, and the leaders of this new organization were Elizabeth Cady Stanton, Susan B. Anthony, Carrie Chapman Catt, Frances Willard, Matilda Joslyn Gage, and Ann Howard Shaw.

Chapter Four

Moving Toward the Vote

T he NAWSA started to take on a life of its own and placed women in the political spotlight. In 1890, Jane Addams and Ellen Gates Starr began Hull House in Chicago. This was a settlement housing project for needy women. Within one year, there were more than 100 of these houses. Nearly all the houses were run by women. This movement put both college-educated white women and women of color into successful careers in social work. These women also became a voice to reckon with in American politics.

In 1895, Elizabeth Cady Stanton published her controversial *The Woman's Bible*. Stanton's book announced that the Bible's teachings degrade women "from Genesis to Revelations." Afraid that Stanton was damaging the NAWSA campaign, many suffragists didn't want to work

Peaceful parades were a popular way to get suffragist voices heard in America. In cities such as Boston, shown here, and smaller towns around the country, parading for the cause made people take notice.

with her. Stanton had resigned as NAWSA president in 1892 (Susan B. Anthony took over) but continued to sit onstage at the conventions. After her book was published, she was no longer invited to the meetings.

Carrie Chapman Catt became president of NAWSA in 1900 and did much for the organization. She spent countless

Anti-suffrage Movement

Not everyone was in support of suffrage. In 1911, the National Association Opposed to Woman Suffrage (NAOWS) was organized and led by Mrs. Arthur Dodge. Its members included wealthy socialite women and some Catholic clergymen.

Helen Kendrick Johnson (1844–1917) was an avid anti-suffragette. In 1897, Johnson wrote a book called *Woman and the Republic*. She used statistics to declare that women did not need the vote to establish legal and other equality. She argued that women should enjoy their separate domestic world. Johnson thought this balance was essential for the American republic.

hours speechmaking, organizing women, and gaining political experience. In 1902, Catt helped organize the International Woman Suffrage Alliance (IWSA), which eventually got support from thirty-two nations.

Anti-suffragettes thought women were too frail to vote. They even thought that by maybe upsetting the different male and female roles, the end of the nation would come. Maybe it would even send America into war. The "antis" also predicted that if women got the vote, they would vote more than once. Before voting machines, voters wrote names on paper and placed the ballot in a box.

THE AWAKENING

Newspaper cartoons showed the opinions of those who wanted voters' rights and those who didn't. This cartoon by Hy Mayer from 1915 shows a woman standing on the western states (which already had voting rights), holding a hand out to women in the East who are reaching out to her.

In 1904, Catt resigned as president of NAWSA to care for her ailing husband but came back in 1915 when many members of the group had become divided under the presidency of Ann Howard Shaw.

It was at this time that Catt revealed her "winning plan" in Atlantic City, New Jersey. At this time, states

Those opposed to women gaining the vote also used cartoons and editorials to show what they thought would happen if women began to vote. The cartoon on the left shows how men's and women's roles would reverse when women gained voting rights. The editorial on the right points out the dangers some believed were awaiting America with women's suffrage.

were still divided on the issue of suffrage. Catt's plan was to campaign simultaneously for suffrage on both the state and federal levels. The second part of the plan was to compromise for partial (or some) suffrage in the states

A President Backs Suffrage

President Woodrow Wilson (1856–1924) did many things besides support suffrage. He steered Congress through three major pieces of legislation. The first was the Underwood Act, which lowered tariffs, or taxes, on products that could be made more cheaply in the United States. Second, the passage of the Federal Reserve Act provided the nation with money that it badly needed. Finally, in 1914, an antitrust legislation established the Federal Trade Commission to stop unfair business practices.

that were against suffrage. Under Catt's leadership, the NAWSA won the backing of the United States House of Representatives and the Senate. She also won state support for the ratification of an amendment giving women the right to vote. In 1917, New York passed a state women's suffrage referendum. By 1918, President Woodrow Wilson was finally won over to the idea of women's suffrage.

On August 26, 1920, the Nineteenth Amendment to the U.S. Constitution was adopted when the state of Tennessee ratified it (made it into law). Tennessee's vote was the final vote needed to grant women full voting rights throughout all the United States. Unfortunately, the pioneers of the

On November 2, 1920, women all across the nation stood in line at the polls for the first time. Their fight to gain recognition had been a long struggle. It took an amendment to the Constitution to help end this discrimination in the country.

movement did not live to see the ratification. Elizabeth Cady Stanton passed away in 1902, and Susan B. Anthony died in 1906. Without them and their determination and hard work, the fight may have been delayed for many years.

In the first election open to women, 8 million women voted. It took 144 years to achieve the equality that

Thomas Jefferson had written about in the Declaration of Independence.

After the passing of the Nineteenth Amendment, Carrie Chapman Catt organized the League of Women Voters, which still exists today. The main mission of this league is to encourage women to become involved in politics. Its first president was Maud Park. In 1924, Park started the Women's Joint Congressional Committee, which helped lobby for an end to child labor. This organization also campaigned for the promotion of maternity aid, health, and welfare programs.

The Progressive movement helped pave the way for much success in women's political-rights battles.

Glossary

abolitionism (ah-bo-LISH-shun-ism) The idea or practice of ending slavery.

ardor (ARH-dur) Extreme passion.

arson (AR-sun) The willful setting of fire to property, especially with criminal intent.

delegates (DEH-lih-gets) Representatives to a conference or convention.

domesticity (doh-mes-TI-si-tee) Relating to the household or family; devoted to home duties or pleasures.

liability (ly-uh-BIL-ih-tee) Something or someone that acts as a disadvantage.

liberty (LIH-ber-tee) Freedom.

morality (muh-RA-luh-tee) A system of conduct that expresses correct behavior.

pacifist (PA-si-fist) Someone who is against war.

piety (PY-ih-tee) Dutifulness in religion.

radical (RAH-dih-kul) To make extreme changes in existing views.

referendum (ref-er-EN-dum) A vote on a measure passed by a legislative body.

resolution (reh-zuh-LOO-shun) A formal expression of opinion or intent voted by an assembled group.

stereotypical (ster-ee-oh-TIH-pi-kul) Conforming to a fixed idea.

suffrage (SUH-frij) The right to vote.

suffragist (SUH-frij-ist) Someone who advocates the voting rights of women.

Web Sites

Due to the changing nature of Internet links, the Rosen Publishing Group, Inc., has developed an online list of Web sites related to the subject of this book. This site is updated regularly. Please use this link to access the list:

http://www.rosenlinks.com/pmnhnt/wosu

Primary Source Image List

Page 7 (left): Title page of "Woman in Her Various Relations," 1853, by Lydia Green Abell. Currently housed at the Smithsonian Institution, Washington, DC.

Page 7 (right): A woman holding a child in her lap, photographed by James Presley Ball between 1847 and 1860. Currently housed at the Library of Congress, Washington, DC.

Page 8: Photograph of Mary Lyon in 1832. Currently housed at the Mount Holyoke College Archives, South Hadley, Massachusetts.

Page 11 (left): Portrait of Lucretia Mott, circa 1870. Currently housed at the Library of Congress, Washington, DC.

Page 11 (right): Portrait of Elizabeth Cady Stanton and Susan B. Anthony, circa 1890. Currently housed at the Library of Congress, Washington, DC.

Page 16: Petition to Congress asking for an amendment to the Constitution for the right to universal suffrage, 1866. Currently housed at the National Archives, Washington, DC.

Page 17: Photograph of state presidents and officers of the National American Woman Suffrage Association, 1892. Currently housed at the Bryn Mawr College library special collections.

Page 21: Photograph of a suffrage parade in Boston, Massachusetts, May 3, 1914. Currently housed at the Schlesinger Library of the History of Women in America, Radcliffe Institute, Boston.

Page 24 (left): Editorial cartoon titled "Election Day!," circa 1909. Currently housed at the Library of Congress, Washington, DC.

Page 24 (right): Anti–women's suffrage poster, circa 1912, from Watertown, Wisconsin. Currently housed at the Wisconsin Historical Society, Madison, Wisconsin.

Index

A
abolition, 8, 12
American Equal Rights Association, 15
American Woman Suffrage Association
    (AWSA), 16–17
Anthony, Susan B., 12, 15, 19, 20–21, 26
anti-suffrage movement, 22

C
Catt, Carrie Chapman, 19, 21–25, 27
Civil War, 6, 14
colleges, 8, 20

D
Declaration of Sentiments, 10–12
Douglass, Frederick, 12, 15

E
Emancipation Proclamation, 14

F
Fifteenth Amendment, 17

G
Gage, Matilda Joslyn, 12, 19
Grimke, Sarah, 8

H
Howe, Julia Ward, 16
Hull House, 20

I
International Woman Suffrage Alliance
    (IWSA), 22

J
Johnson, Helen Kendrick, 22

L
League of Women Voters, 27
Lincoln, Abraham, 14
Lyon, Mary, 8

M
Married Woman's Property Act, 8
Mott, Lucretia, 9–10, 15
Mount Holyoke College, 8

N
National American Woman Suffrage
    Association (NAWSA), 19, 20–22,
    23, 25
National Woman Suffrage Association
    (NWSA), 15–16, 17
Nineteenth Amendment, 4, 25, 27
North Star, 12

O
Oberlin College, 8

P
Park, Maud, 27
Progressive movement, 5, 27

R
reforms, 5–6, 12
Ruffin, Josephine, 16

S
settlement houses, 20
Shaw, Ann Howard, 19, 23
slavery/slaves, 8, 9, 12, 14, 17
Stanton, Elizabeth Cady, 9–10, 12, 15, 19,
    20–21, 26
Stone, Lucy, 15, 16

About the Author

Jennifer MacBain-Stephens lives and writes in California.